# On the Sofa

By Marcus Jormin

Foreword

Before you get all confused from reading this book, don't say I didn't warn you about how weird it'd be. This is the result of what happens if you give Marcus Jormin a paper and pen without further instructions. His creativity (if you can call it that) sparks genuine concern and confusion, sometimes to the point where you feel like you're out of this world. Ok let me stop spitting out random words and get you to the real juice. The juice which is sometimes (barely) logical, and sometimes pure senseless stuff (that you only can make true sense of grammatically), and everything in between. It's written by Marcus Jormin, and that guy is me. Hi.

Enjoy

MJ

When I was young, I got a suntan. The next day I didn't want to look like I'd been a bad boy by not wearing sunscreen. So before I went to school I tried to brush the tan off with a broom.

I heard my neighbors were expecting a baby. It had been a year since, so I figured they'd have it. But when I asked about it, they said they fed it with the wrong fuel so it had to be scrapped.

I once filmed a police car chasing a bus. At the bus stop, the police didn't break on time, so the car bashed into the back of the bus. The cop jumped out of the driver's seat and told me: Post it on Instagram and I'll appreciate you.

Isn't it ironic that people who die from falling trees are either environmentalists or just plain stupid?

Which type of person has a hilarious IQ of 200, but an intelligence IQ of 50?
People who pee in their pants and wear them backwards to hide it.

I entered the wrong classroom, and it turned out it was a teacher's meeting. No wonder everyone got straight Fs.

Tell me something that's not true without telling me that it's not true.
I drew with Usain Bolt in a 100m sprint.

An eagle flew down to me, and I got so scared so I threw a marble at it and it landed in its mouth. It choked and tumbled down before me. I bought a lottery ticket the same day, but my dog ate it.

My dream has always been to fly through the rain forest by dodging the trees, just so sloths can feel fast.

My friend had a horse, and it needed a makeover. I didn't know you could just paint a horse like that.

Ever since the President of the United States hit me in my dreams, I've been waking up wondering why I'd hurt myself like that. It haunts me until I realize that I'm not actually the President of the United States.

At the amusement park I wanted some variety for once, so I agreed to be taken on a new ride. It was hell and not fair to anyone. Surely they had tested it before. They must have.

Building a hamster out of lego was fun. When it was done, I got up to take a photo of it. I stepped on it and started to bleed. I kicked it and started to bleed even more. At least it got shattered into pieces but my wall also started to bleed. I got a real hamster that bit me. Way better alternative.

I was printing a picture of an apple, but I was out of color. Luckily a butterfly flew into the printer and got grinded, so its blood colored the apple. Great life hack! It's free, realistic (since the blood will turn brown later, just like a rotting apple), and the apple got a worm inside of it. Or should I say caterpillar?

The worst part about being a substitute teacher is that you have absolutely no idea about the subject you're teaching. If you get thrown into a sewing class where the students are in the middle of a weaving project, it's best for you to just sit down and say "Today you will be continuing the assignment that you have", and then just sit down because you don't know how to do it yourself. Maybe it's quite a good thing actually since you get paid for it.

An actual project that I had once in school was to fold a piece of paper as much as possible, and then try to straighten it out again. This is, of course, impossible, just as if you were to bully someone and then expect them to be normal again some time. What a scandal.

What if there was a bomb that you could set to detonate in a million years. Actually, what if someone's already done it? We could be living in one gigantic minefield.

What if a broken light bulb is just a bug in our eyes that makes our brains interpret it as being turned off.

When it starts to rain just as you step out the door, it's really got to mean something about that nature has something against you.

When curtain rods fall down, remember it could've been worse. Like a clock would be worse, say. It all depends on what you had underneath.

Is a prison like a private zoo for the guards who work there? Gosh, that's genuinely a very disturbing thought. Well, at least in some countries.

People are able to build houses with their bare hands. It's like an everyday thing to do for them. Low key, that's the coolest thing a human can do. Name a cooler ability and I'll wait.

I love the smell of laundry. Powdered detergent is dangerous. Not because it looks like coke, but because it will kill you faster than coke.

What if there was a Nobel stress prize?

There are so many types of golf. You could turn any sport into golf. Imagine if you'd do it with yourself. That's a new Olympic long jump event.

I don't fully understand people who like to be in nature. Couldn't a bear just come and have you for dinner?

I'd like to see wax figures with realistic insides.

Isn't it weird that literally anything wrapped in aluminum foil looks like a cake? Wrap your shoe in it and the next thing you know you're eating it because you thought it was a cake. People make cake art anyways so whenever I see something on social media I always wait for when the knife comes out and cuts it in half to reveal that it's actually cake.

A job I applied for required that you were a woman. I got so far in the application process, so they didn't know that I was a man until I got to the interview.

Talkative people who interrupt talking to talkative people are worse than the talkative people they interrupt.

Love always wins, unless it makes you lose.
Then it always loses.

Robots are so modern and cool. So much so that
their intellectual electronic signals in their brains
are so strong, so they shock you. Stop talking to
robots and talk to a normal person, you lonely
one.

I got a huge deal for a magazine app. However,
in their magazine they had material that
required you to have the physical magazine. So I
got the actual physical magazine for its normal
price. I am so smart! Be like me.

Installing a rooster on my roof in a completely normal neighborhood was so fun. My neighbors thought I had it as a pet until they found out that I had it just to wake them up with it. It wasn't even real, you see. Just a prank bro.

Do lasers go through invisible people? Can someone try that out and get back to me? Thanks

Why not use an entire house as a storage unit? Yeah definitely, why not? You just go right ahead.

In the future, I'm gonna invent a hammer that shatters itself when you give it to a baby. Doing so would mean I first need to finish what I'm inventing now. I can't really reveal what that is, but it has something to do with preventing shards from stabbing a baby.

My mixed opinions make people so jealous. I don't know why.

What if sending messages to space turns out to be the worst decision ever. People are too scared to send messages on their phones so why is it ok to send them into space? You won't find your new partner there. I promise just text them and make the first move already.

Retiring frightens me. I don't want to be at a retirement home if I retire at 30.

One should tell 8-up to stop outsourcing Sprite.

Everyone has a laptop, if you think about it. Actually maybe not...

I don't understand why guys sometimes do a "spontaneous workout" by flexing muscles when they see a girl. Like come on, where did you even get that dumbbell from? Your head!

I need to try sitting in a freight train and eating burgers at the same time.

Penguins are such cool birds. I'm happy they can't just fly away when you hug one.

Now that I think about it, the front row at the movies isn't so bad after all.

What if you made up your own dialect to your kid, so they started speaking some sort of maximum authority speech.

A bird playing the guitar is cool. The noise of their beak leaving each pick on the string is so satisfying. Use your guitar as a bird feeder!

I enjoy looking at my own Instagram posts with my alter egos.

People debate all the time about what place serves the best coffee. Keep doing that by all means! As long as we all agree that the best toast is the one you make at home. Noone except yourself can become a successful toast chef.

Is it just me, or do Italians get mad very mildly?

A customizable necklace that changes color depending on your mood is so cool. We've come so far it's such a great time to be alive.

If you bother me when I tell you to not bother me, I'll join you next time on your date.

Sometimes I stretch in the attic to flex on the ghosts with my body.

If a church is blue, that's so heaven.

I want needles on my car seats, so I can drive safely. We all have our preferences so don't judge me until you've tried. You don't even know what kind of needles I'm talking about.

Let's ask a real camera person why they don't help the people they're filming.

Mark my words. Sometime you'll be able to print stuff from your phone. Just load it with paper and boom. Photography!

It really is nice to just take some moments sometimes to appreciate that you don't have a cold. It makes you feel better instantly.

The weirdest thing that's ever happened to me while I've been out for a walk is that a goat randomly appeared running on the road. I guess it had escaped because whoever owned it probably cared for it a lot, since it had such a nice beard. I used it as a dog.

It helps to increase your discipline on the field as goalkeeper if you think about the "fans" who'll murder the other fans if you let a goal in.

I've still never fully understood why you'd buy dirt when there is dirt already all around you.

A guy pranked me once by pretending to be a mannequin. That was cool and all, but the coolest thing is that I really don't understand how the other people in the mannequins manage to stand so still all day.

Exercising in space must make it so much easier to lift heavy and run far. Become an astronaut, and you'll become a world class athlete at the same time.

Could anyone who's worked as one of Santa's elves message me and tell me what it's like?

I appreciate all moms out there, for going through such terrible conditions to give birth to us.